W9-BLA-958

Body Books

Brain

Anna Sandeman
Illustrated by Ian Thompson

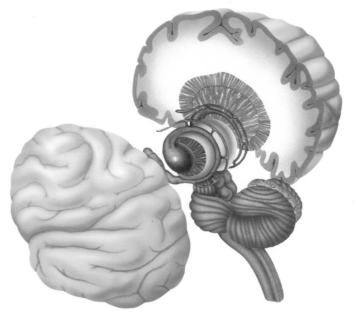

COPPER BEECH BOOKS
BROOKFIELD, CONNECTICUT

Copyright © 1996 Aladdin Books Ltd.
Produced by Aladdin Books Limited
28 Percy Street
London W1P 0LD

Designed by: David West Children's
Book Design
Designer: Edward Simkins
Editor: Liz White
Picture Research: Brooks Krikler Research
Consultants: Dr. R. Levene, M.D.
Jan Bastoncino, Dip. Ed.

First published in
the United States in 1996 by
Copper Beech Books,
an imprint of The Millbrook Press
2 Old New Milford Road
Brookfield, Connecticut 06804

Printed in Belgium
All rights reserved

Library of Congress Cataloging-in-Publication Data
Sandeman, Anna.
Brain / by Anna Sandeman; illustrated by Ian Thompson.
p. cm.–(Body books)
Includes index
Summary: Describes the functions of the brain as the control
system of the body and the nervous system, with a focus on
learning and remembering as well as problems that can occur
within the brain.
ISBN 0-7613-0490-8 (lib. bdg.)
1. Brain–Physiology–Juvenile literature. [1. Brain] I.
Thompson, Ian, 1964- ill. II. Title. III. Series:
Sandeman, Anna. Body books.
QP376.3316 1996
612.8'2–dc20   96-13907
CIP AC
Photocredits: Abbreviations: t-top, m-
middle, b-bottom, r-right, l-left
All the photos in this book are by
Roger Vlitos except: 16tr & 28l
Frank Spooner Pictures; 21t Hulton
Deutsch Collection; 22t & 26tr Science
Photo Library; 28-29 Bruce Coleman
Collection.   5 4 3

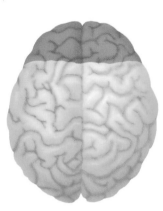

Contents

Human brain

Who has a brain? All animals

with backbones have a brain. The sperm whale has the largest brain of all, weighing up to 20 pounds (9 kg) – the weight of a nine-month-old baby. An elephant's brain weighs 11 pounds (5 kg), while a mouse's brain weighs only a few ounces.

An adult human brain weighs about three and a half pounds – slightly less than a large bag of flour. Compared with a whale's brain this is small. But compared with the size of the human body, it is big.

Brain size alone does not show how clever or stupid an animal is. This is true for humans, too. Most men have heavier brains than women, but this does not mean they are more intelligent.

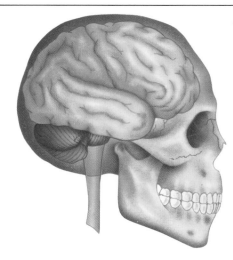

Your brain

Your brain fills the upper half of your head. It is like a soft, pinkish-gray wrinkled sponge. More than three quarters of it is made of water. Without a skull to support and protect your brain, it would sag like jelly.

The brain is made up of three main parts. The largest of these, the cerebrum, is divided into two walnut-shaped halves. The cerebrum is the thinking part of the brain. It allows you to move how you want, to solve problems, and to remember.

Cerebrum

Cerebrum

Cerebellum

Brain stem

Below the cerebrum, at the back of the brain, is the cerebellum. This makes sure your body muscles work together smoothly. It also helps you to keep your balance. The brain stem helps to control how your body machine works. Among other things, it is partly responsible for your heartbeat, your breathing, and the digestion of your food.

The nervous system

Together the three areas of your brain control how your body works by receiving and sending signals to different parts of it. The signals travel along bundles of fine hairlike threads called nerves.

Some signals travel straight to the brain. Most pass first through the spinal cord – a long bundle of nerves inside your backbone, or spine. Like your brain, your spinal cord is more than three quarters water.

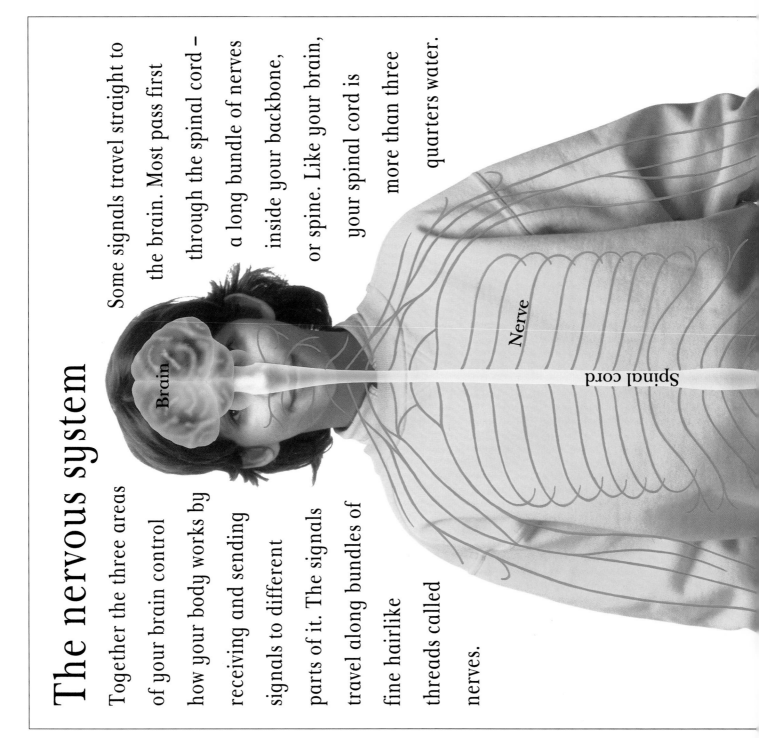

Brain

Nerve

Spinal cord

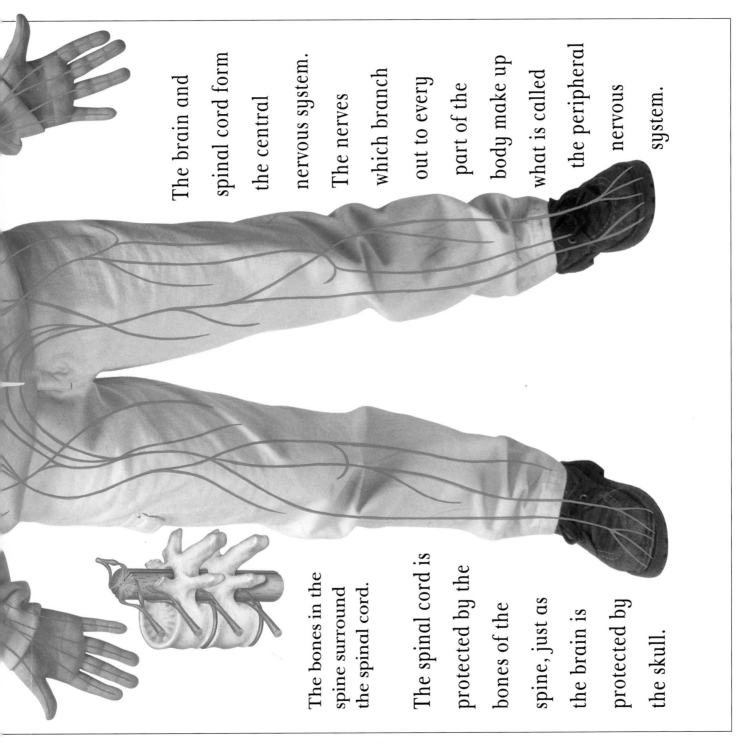

The brain and spinal cord form the central nervous system. The nerves which branch out to every part of the body make up what is called the peripheral nervous system.

The bones in the spine surround the spinal cord.

The spinal cord is protected by the bones of the spine, just as the brain is protected by the skull.

Nerve signals

A wasp is about to land on your hand. What do you do?

First your eyes send a warning signal to your brain. Your brain immediately sends another signal back to your muscles, telling them to move your hand. Your brain decides exactly how your hand should move.

Movements like these are called voluntary movements.

The green arrows show the direction of the nerve signals.

Some movements, which happen very quickly without your thinking about them, are called reflexes. For example, if you touch a hot saucepan the signal is flashed from your hand to your brain telling it how hot the pan is. A signal is sent immediately to the muscles of the arm telling them to pull your hand away.

Your tendons also have reflexes. Try to test them. Sit with your legs crossed and get a friend to tap your knee just below the kneecap. Your leg will kick. The sensors between your knee tendon and leg muscles send messages to the spinal cord. The message comes back telling your leg to straighten.

The cerebrum

Most of the muscles that move your head, body, and limbs work only when you want them to. They are called voluntary muscles. They are controlled by the cortex, the outer layer of the cerebrum.

Unlike animals, humans have a wrinkled cortex with deep folds. If it were unfolded, the cortex would cover an area 30 times as big. The cortex is divided into many areas which receive and transmit different signals.

The voluntary muscles are controlled by an area running across the two halves of the cerebrum. This is called the motor area.

Thinking

Speaking

If you feel a mosquito land on your leg, your skin sends a signal to one small part of your cortex. This area then passes on the information to your motor area, which sends a signal down to the muscles in your leg, telling it to move.

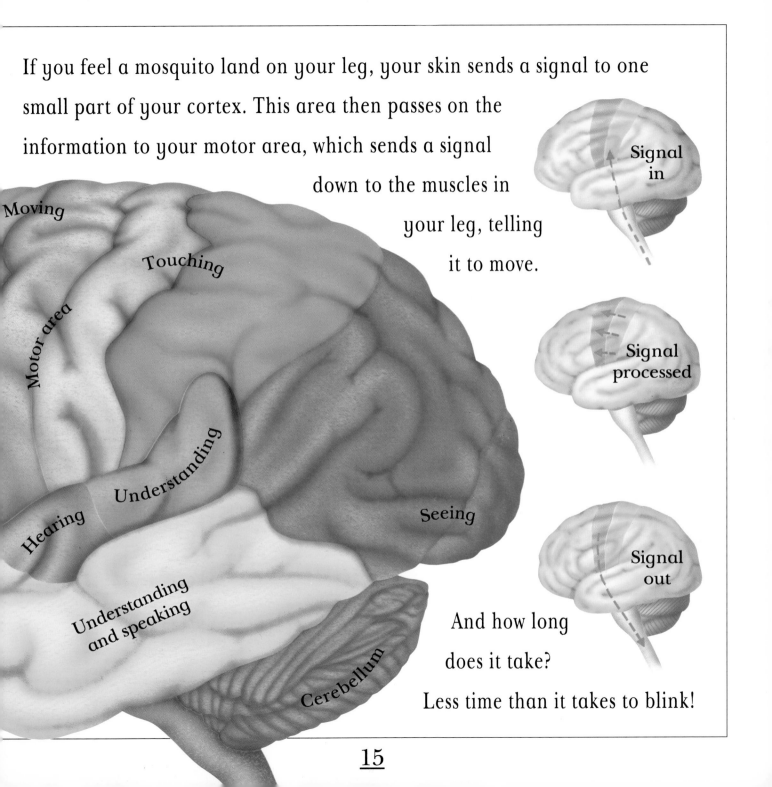

Moving

Touching

Motor area

Understanding

Hearing

Seeing

Understanding and speaking

Cerebellum

Signal in

Signal processed

Signal out

And how long does it take?
Less time than it takes to blink!

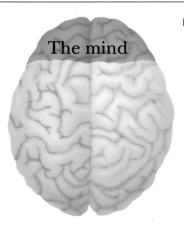

The mind

The mind

At the front of the cerebrum is the area used for thinking. This area is normally called the mind.

Each half of your brain seems to do different kinds of thinking. Usually, the right side is used for feelings and imagination. You use it when you paint, write a story, or play make-believe games.

The left side is normally used for talking and for understanding speech. It is also used to solve problems – to add up your allowance, for example, or to build a model.

Have you ever wondered how a newborn foal knows it must struggle to its feet and drink its mother's milk? It knows what to do by instinct, without being taught.

When you were a baby, your mind was almost a blank. You knew how to suck and how to cry. You did both by instinct.

But as you grew, your mind soaked up more and more information about the world around you. You began to learn, and your mind developed.

Learning

How do you learn? Like other parts of your body, most of your nervous system is made up of millions of tiny cells. These cells are called neurons. All neurons have a body. Each has a long "tail," or nerve fiber, linking it to other neurons, muscles, or other parts of your body. Some nerve fibers are less than an inch long. Others can stretch up to three feet (1m) – from your spinal cord to your big toe!

Each neuron also has lots of branches sprouting from its center. Nerve fibers from other neurons are attached to these branches. This means that every neuron is linked to thousands of other neurons.

When you start to learn something, signals pass from one neuron to another, over and over again, along a path. Think back to when you learned how to ride a bicycle. Remember how hard it was at first to steer straight and to keep your balance? But with practice – after the same signal had traveled the same path countless times – you could ride with ease.

As you grow up and your knowledge increases, more and more pathways are used. But after the age of 25 or so your neurons start to die – and no new ones grow to take their place. This is why older people find it harder to learn than children.

??? Memory

Can you remember your name? Of course! Now try to remember what you ate for lunch exactly a week ago. Not so easy, is it?

Without memory you could not learn anything. It is thought that there are two types of memory – a long-term memory and a short-term memory.

Things that you learn early are kept in your long-term memory. These include facts (such as your name and address), actions (for example, how to brush your teeth), and even sights, sounds, smells, and tastes. Strong feelings, too, are kept in your long-term memory.

You use your short-term memory to store things which happened a few minutes or hours ago.

Try playing the shopping game. Start by saying, "I'm going shopping to buy some bread." The next person continues, "I'm going shopping to buy some bread and some apples," and so on.

How long is the list before somebody forgets something?

Many older people find it hard to remember things which happened a short time ago. Yet they can often remember events which took place when they were young. See if your grandparents can remember their first day of school. Can you?

I'm going shopping to buy some bread and...

Sleep

Even when you are asleep, millions of signals are being sent back and forth inside your brain. Doctors can measure the number and speed of these signals with a special machine. The machine displays the signals as patterns of wavy lines (sometimes called brain waves). This display is called an EEG. Doctors use EEGs to help them find out what is wrong with a patient's brain.

The wave patterns change as your brain becomes more or less active. When you are awake and thinking hard, the waves are small and spiky.

When you are relaxed (while you are watching television, for example), the waves are taller and wider.

When you are asleep, the waves are very large and long. During sleep, you may dream. No one knows what dreams are for. Many people think they are the brain's way of sorting out information it has received during the day. Anything important is stored in the memory. Everything else is allowed to fade away.

The cerebellum

Your cerebellum is only one eighth the size of your cerebrum, but without it you wouldn't be able to do any but the simplest movements. You couldn't even pat your head, or rub your tummy.

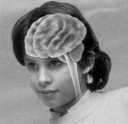

Your cerebellum also helps you to keep your balance and to stand up straight. Without a cerebellum tightrope walking would be impossible!

Next time you are standing on a bus or train, notice how your legs automatically bend and straighten to keep your body upright.

The brain stem

Your brain stem attaches your brain to your spinal cord. It helps to control muscles in your body over which your mind has no power. If you are exercising, it tells your lungs to breathe more deeply; if you have just eaten breakfast, it tells your stomach to start digesting.

Your brain stem also sifts through the millions of signals sent to the brain every second from the rest of your body. Only important signals are let through so that your brain doesn't get confused.

Looking after your
brain
Like all parts of your body, your brain needs to be treated with care. Injuries and diseases can cause damage. These can be serious when brain cells are destroyed as the body cannot replace them.

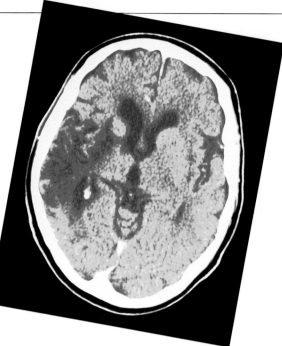

Doctors use a CAT scanner to look at the brain. The CAT takes a picture of your brain. It beams X rays through the head and the results appear on a computer screen.

The hard, thick bones of your skull help to protect your brain against any bumps, but you can also do certain things to protect your brain. One obvious precaution is to wear a helmet when cycling or playing dangerous sports.

Less obviously, taking care of your body generally will also help to keep your brain in good working order.

Have you noticed that when you are tired it is difficult to think clearly? Your brain works much better if you have had enough rest.

Exercise and a healthy diet help your brain to work at its best.

Did you know?

... that if your cortex were smoothed out it would have the surface area of a pillowcase?

... that a cat's cerebellum is much larger for its body than a human's is? This is why it can move so quickly and balance so well.

... that nerve messages travel at very different speeds? They vary between one and a half feet, and 400 feet per second – faster than a high-speed train.

... that the nerves in a grown-up's body stretch for 47 miles?

... that your brain equals about one fiftieth of your body weight, but uses one fifth of your body's energy supply?

... that during a lifetime of 70 years a person spends about 186,000 hours asleep? A fifth of that time is spent dreaming.

... that *Stegosaurus* measured up to 33 feet in length, but had a brain no bigger than a golf ball?

Glossary

Cerebellum – The part of the brain that aids balance and helps your muscles to work together

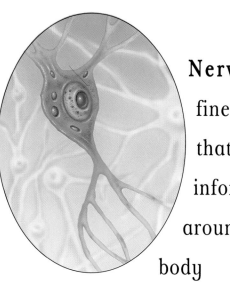

Nerve – A long fine thread that carries information around the body

Cerebrum – The large front part of the brain that helps you to think, move, and remember

Cortex – The wrinkled, outer surface of the brain

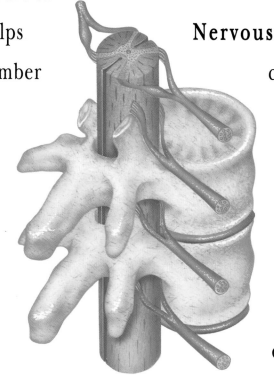

Nervous system – The collective name for the brain, spinal cord, and nerves

Mind – The area at the front of the cerebrum used for thinking

Spinal cord – A long bundle of nerves

Index

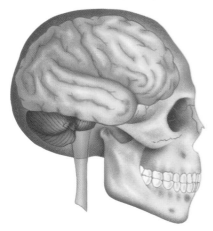
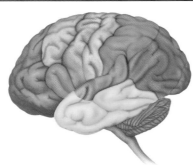
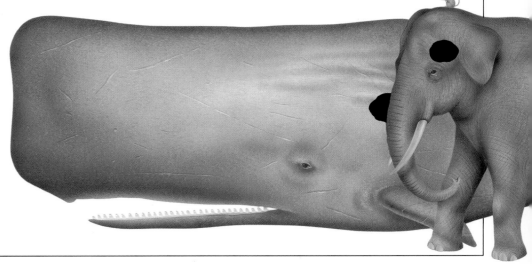